Winter Art-Contents

D1073626

Snowball Chain

Each of these fellows is dressed uniquely for winter. The snowballs are what tie them all together.

Materials:
- Reproduce the pattern below.
- Construction paper cut in 4¼" x 22" strip

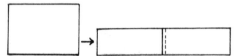

- Scissors and crayons

Steps to follow:

1. Fold your paper back and forth to match the width of the pattern (2½").

2. Lay the pattern on the top of the folded paper and cut on the dotted lines.

3. Open your chain and use crayons to creatively dress each paper doll in its own wonderful winter wear.

4. Outline the snowball with black crayon. To make them really stand out, put a ring of glue around the snowball and sprinkle with glitter.

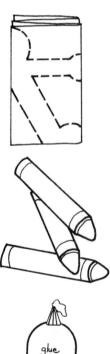

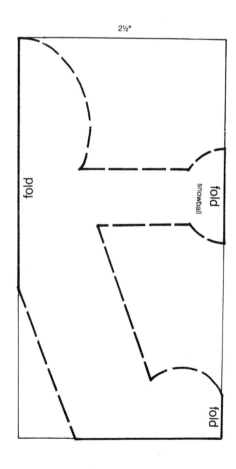

A Hibernating Bear
Where did he go?

Here is a quick and easy way to enliven a class study of animal winter habitats.

Materials:
White construction paper
9" x 12"
Crayons, pencil

Steps to follow:

1. Begin by folding the white construction paper.

2. Sketch in details in pencil first. Then add color. Draw the hill and entrance to the den (or burrow) on the top portion of your folded paper. Open the paper and draw the sleeping bear (or other hibernating animal) inside.

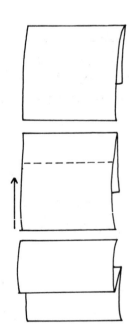

Positive-Negative Trees

Experimenting with different tree shapes helps widen your students' awareness of the variations in nature.
Developing a positive-negative design is fun and the contrast is striking.

Materials:
- Construction paper
    - White 12 x 18 — background
    - Blue 6 x 18 — sky
- Scissors, pencil and paste

Steps to follow:

Before beginning, display a wide variety of tree outline shapes on the chalkboard.

1. Lay the blue paper on the top half of the white paper.

    Sketch a line of tree shapes with your pencil. The base of the tree must come to the lower edge of the blue paper. You may use all one shape or many variations. Trees don't need to be the same height.

2. Cut out the trees following your pencil line.

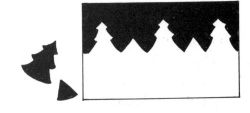

3. Paste the blue sky paper to the top half of your white background paper (WITHOUT the cut-out trees).

    Now lay the trees back in their original spots. Put paste on the backs (one tree at a time) and carefully flip the tree down to form a shadow for the white tree. Be sure the base lines line up. Paste the rest of the tree shadows down.

Animal Tracks
Who made them?

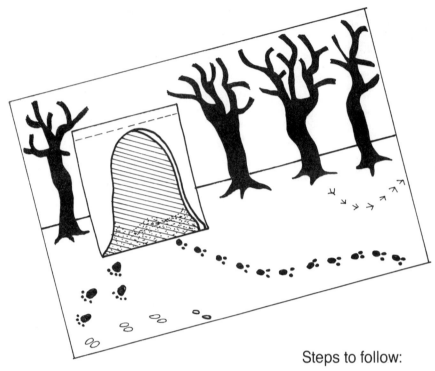

Use your school library as a resource for discovering types of animal tracks. Encyclopedias usually have a whole section devoted to this topic. You may use this activity as a motivation for writing exciting stories about what the tracker is about to discover.

Materials:
White construction paper
    12″ x 18″ background
    4″ x 4″ flap
Crayons, pencils with erasers
Paste
Black tempera plus fingers

Steps to follow:

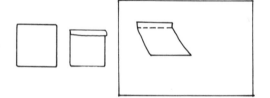

1. Fold down a ½″ flap on the 4″ x 4″ paper. Paste this flap to the background sheet. Think about what animals have left tracks in the snow.

2. Use crayon to draw the bare winter trees. Draw a black horizon line. Draw the entrance to a cave on the flap. Color it.

3. Lift the cave flap. Draw an animal underneath.

4. Now use your fingers or the eraser on a pencil to print rows of tracks on your paper. Dip your fingers (or pencil eraser) into the black paint and then print on the paper. Remember what you learned about tracks in your encyclopedia.
Invent a story about what happened to all the creatures that made these tracks.

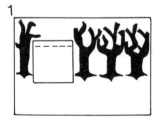

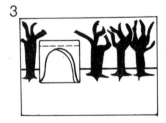

Toboggan Kids

This art lesson can be used on a bulletin board with great success or to add interest to creative stories about winter fun.

Materials:
Reproduce the pattern on the following page on white construction paper.
Brown construction paper
8" x 3½" — toboggan
Crayons
Scissors
Paste

Steps to follow:

1. Color all pattern pieces.
   Draw faces.
   Design sweaters or jackets.
   Add designs to scarves and caps

2. Cut out all pieces. Paste a hat and scarf to each person.

3. Curl end of toboggan
   (A pencil is good for this.)

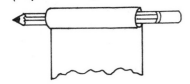

4. Fold the bottom piece of each child under. Fold the arms up. Paste the hands of the front kid to the toboggan. Paste the hands of the back kid to the back of the front kid.

Bulletin board:

Cover the board with blue paper. Attach strips of white butcher paper loosely to the board to form toboggan runs. Tape or glue toboggans to the snow runs.

Pattern for Toboggan Kids

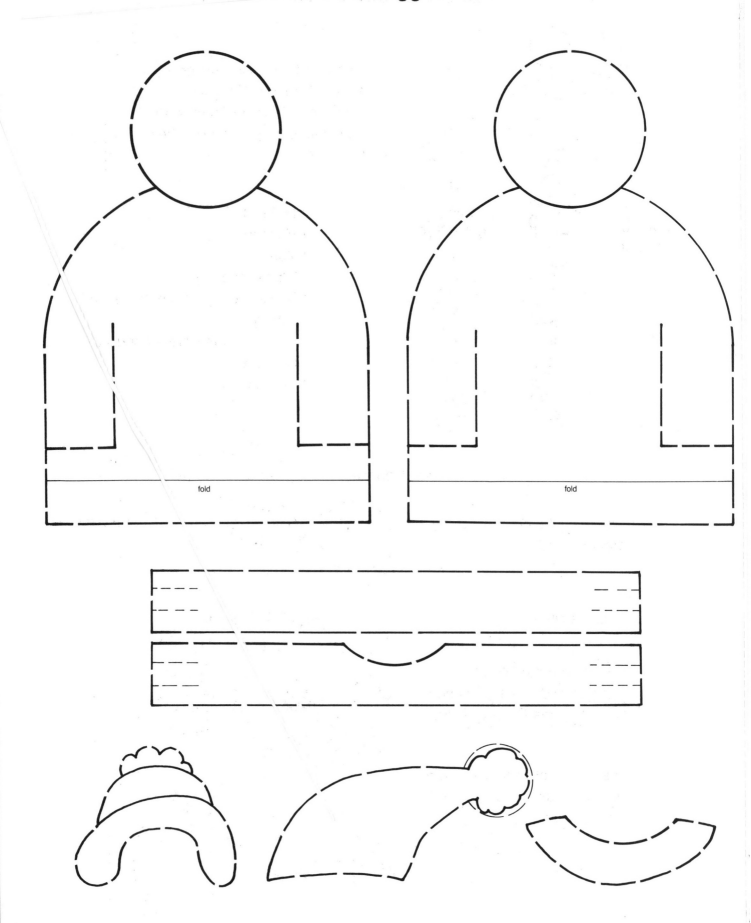

fold

fold

10

WINTER ART

Snowflake Mobiles

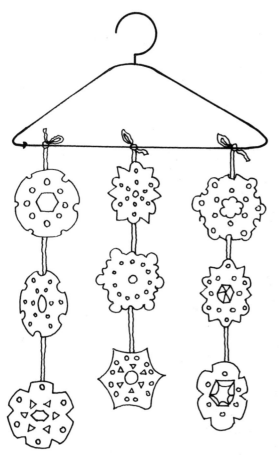

Bring the beauty of a winter snowfall indoors. Hang lacy snowflakes in your windows or from your ceiling and enjoy their movement.

Materials:
- Hangers
- Yarn
- White paper squares
- Use lightweight paper for ease in cutting.
- 4" x 4" squares are a good size.
- Scissors
- Hole punch

Steps to follow:

1. Round off the corners to create a circle.

2. Fold the circle.

3. Create your design with scissors and/or a hole punch. Open the finished snowflake.

4. Paste several snowflakes to a length of yarn. Tie yarn to a clothes hanger.

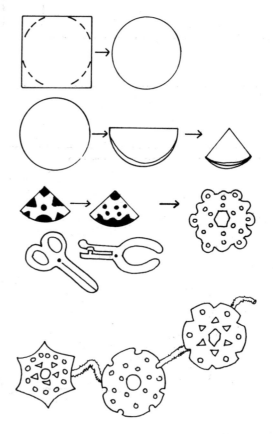

Christmas Design Fun

This project offers the excitement of experimenting with contrasting colors and interesting shapes to create pleasing designs. A small version may be used as a greeting card. Larger forms may be displayed in a quilt-like design on a bulletin board. Colors and shapes can be selected to fit a specific season or holiday.

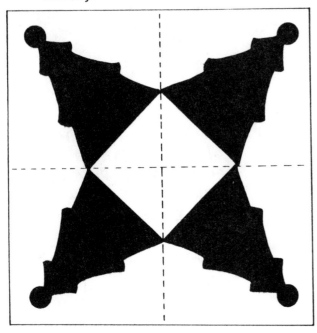

Materials:
- White construction paper 12″ x 12″
- Templates in various designs cut from 6″ squares of tagboard
- Green Construction paper cut ¼ the size of the white 6″ x 6″
- Red paper scraps
- Scissors, paste, pencil, crayon

Steps to follow:

1. Create templates out of tagboard. Use simple shapes appropriate to the season.
2. Chose one template. Trace around it on four green squares. Cut out on the trace lines.
3. Fold the white paper into quarters.
4. Arrange the green shapes around the center of the white paper. Place one shape in each quarter section. Paste in place.
5. Cut small design shapes from red paper and add to the design.
   Use crayons to add final details.

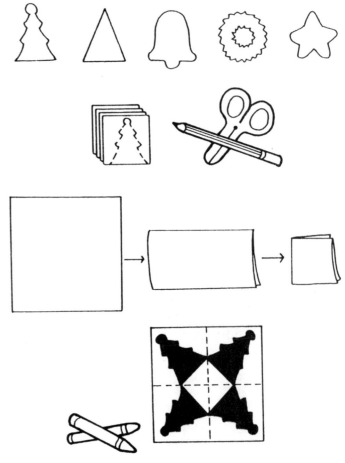

Stencil Your Own Wrapping Paper

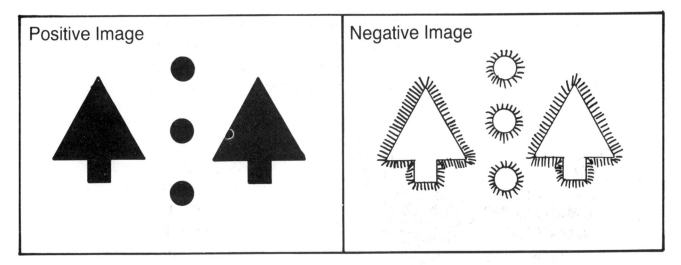

Positive Image

Negative Image

Practice design skills as you learn how to use stencil techniques in creating your own wrapping paper. This activity stresses:

1. development (by teacher and/or students) of a workable stencil pattern.
2. planning a pleasing design.
3. learning that each stencil pattern has a negative and positive image.

Materials:
- Tag squares 4″ x 4″ for cutting stencils
- Exacto knife, scissors
- Paint, crayons or colored pencils
- Paint brushes, sponges, or toothbrushes
- Large sheets of newsprint

Steps to follow:

1. Cut a stencil design. Something simple works best. Save both parts.
2. Select the medium you wish to use: paint, crayons, pencils.
3. Creating a positive image: Use the tag square. Place the stencil on your paper and fill in the empty area with color. (If you use paint, lift the stencil carefully to avoid smears.) Place the stencil in a new position. Repeat until the design is complete.
4. Creating a negative image: Use the cut-out pattern. Using crayon, pencil or paint (a toothbrush works well), brush color out from the edges of the stencil. Lift the stencil and place in a new position. Repeat until the design is complete.
5. You may also try combining the negative and positive images to create an interesting design.

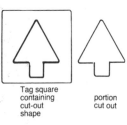

Tag square containing cut-out shape

portion cut out

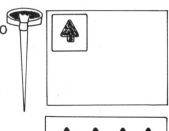

Lace A Stocking

Steps to follow:

1. Cut out the two stockings (for front and back).
2. Plan your design. Then decorate the stocking.

   What can you do?

Cut Paper	Paint	Crayon
stripes	sponge	create red
dots	& paint	and green
your name	finger–	designs
zigzags	paints	
	water	
	colors	

Create the same design on the front and back of the stocking.

3. Punch holes around the stockings about 1″ apart. (Do both stockings at the same time, so the holes will line up for lacing.)
4. Lace the front and back pieces together. Pull the yarn through the needle and begin at the top of the stocking. Tie a knot around the first hole. Now lace around the stocking. Tie a knot at the end.
5. Hang your stocking up to be admired.

Your students can produce colorful Christmas stockings while they practice their coordination skills. Finished stockings can be stuffed with a "surprise" or used to hold Christmas stories or messages.

Materials:
- Reproduce the stocking pattern on card stock or construction paper (two per child).
- Needle
- Paper scraps, paint , or crayons
- Yarn (36″ per stocking)
- Scissors and paste
- Hole punch

Reindeer Card Holder

This project makes a lovely Christmas present to send home for Mom. It is a colorful way to collect all those Christmas cards that arrive in the mail.

Materials:
- Red butcher paper
    17" x 34"
- Construction paper
    brown 7" x 12" — body
        5" x 3" — ears
    black 6" x 8" — antlers
                and eyes
    green 7" x 3" — halter
    red 2½" x 2½" — nose
- Yarn (optional)
- Scissors, paste, stapler
- Hanger

Steps to follow:

1. Staple the red butcher paper to the hanger.
2. Fold up the bottom three times in 4" segments. Staple the edges to create a pocket.
3. Cut out the reindeer pieces and paste to the butcher paper so the reindeer's head is just below the hanger hook.

    Use the black paper scraps to cut out eyes.

    The nose can be extra special if you...
    a. put a spacer behind the red circle to make it stand out.
    b. cut the red circle larger. Cut in and overlap to make a cone-shaped nose.
    c. make a red yarn pompom that's fun to rub.

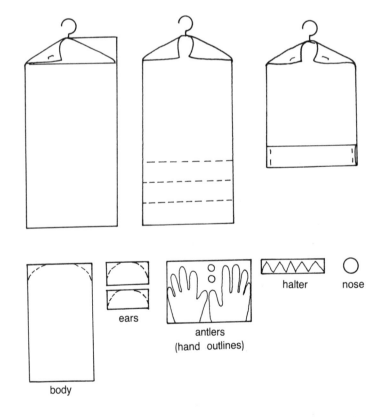

Christmas Banners

words only

words and pictures

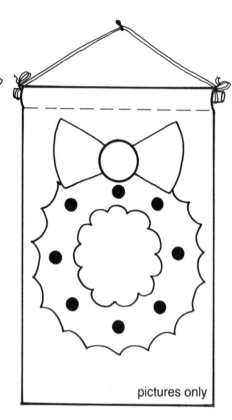

pictures only

Hang these cheerful banners in windows, on doors, or on your front porch to wish a merry time to family and friends.

Materials:
- Butcher paper
    - 18″ x 36″ — narrow banner
    - 24″ x 36″ — wide banner
- Doweling, bamboo plant support, twig . . . to hold banner
- Construction paper in assorted colors
- Paste or glue
- Scissors
- Yarn
- Letter templates

Steps to follow:

Spend some time discussing possible designs, words to use, appropriate pictures, and techniques for tracing and cutting letters or how to create "fat" letters using marking pens. Children may choose to make a preliminary sketch on scratch paper before beginning finished project.

1. Fold both ends of butcher paper over twice (about 2 inch folds). Paste or staple bottom fold.

2. Cut out pieces for banner from construction paper. Arrange entire design on butcher paper. When satisfied with the look, paste the pieces down.

3. Attach doweling to top of banner with paste or staples. Add yarn and hang.

Sleigh and Reindeer

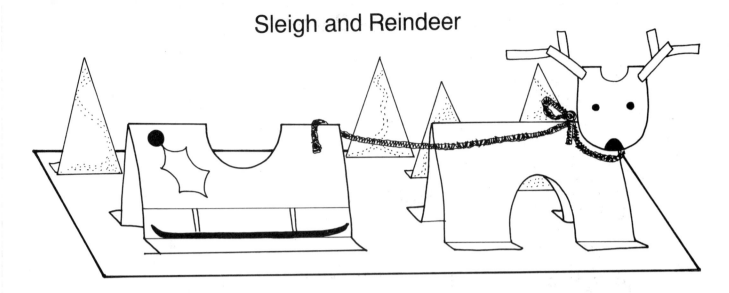

Create a delightful three-dimensional scene to display for Christmas.

Materials:
- Construction paper
    - white 9″ x 12″ — background
    - red 7″ x 4″ — sleigh
    - brown 6″ x 3½″ — reindeer
- Scissors, paste
- Crayons, pencil, yarn

Steps to follow:
1. Sleigh
    a. Fold the red paper in half. Cut out a half circle on the fold.
       Fold up the two bottom edges.
    b. Sketch the sleigh with your pencil on front and back sides. Outline the sleigh and runners with black crayon. Why not decorate the sleigh with some green holly?

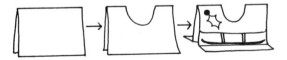

2. Reindeer
    a. Fold the brown paper in half. Cut out a half circle from the open sides. Save the ⌂ for the reindeer's head. Fold up the bottom of the reindeer's feet.
    b. Paste one of the cut out ⌂ to the body. Cut out a small curve from the top to form ears. Use the remaining brown scrap to create antlers. Paste to the reindeer's head.
       Use crayons to add facial features.

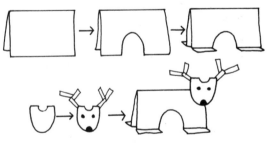

3. Paste the bottom folds of the sleigh and reindeer to the white background paper.
   Tie a loop of yarn around the reindeer's neck. Attach the other end to the sleigh.
4. You may want to add green pine trees.

Rudolph Pop-Up Card

Create very special greeting cards to surprise and delight your friends at Christmas time.

Materials:
- Reproduce the pattern on the following page on construction paper.
- Construction paper 6" x 8" (any color) for folder
- Crayons
- Scissors, paste

Steps to follow:

1. Color reindeer brown with a red nose.

2. Cut out reindeer pieces. Paste ears and antlers to reindeer's head.

3. Prepare pop-up patterns.
   Form A:
   a. Cut out the basic form.
   b. Fold in half. Cut on dotted lines.
   c. Fold back the
   d. Open the paper and push the tab to the reverse side.

   Form B:
   a. Cut out the form.
   b. Cut on dotted line.
   c. Fold on fold lines.
   d. Open and reverse folds by pushing them inside.

4. Putting card together:

   a. Fold construction paper in half to create outside folder.
   b. Put paste around outside edges of Form A. Paste inside folder. Be sure the folder edges meet securely.
   c. Put paste around outside edges of Form B. Paste inside folder, over Form A. Be sure the folded edges meet securely.
   d. Put paste on the tab front. Attach reindeer to the tab. Be sure the bottom of the reindeer touches the fold line.

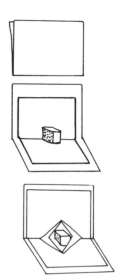

Pattern for the Rudolph Pop-up Card

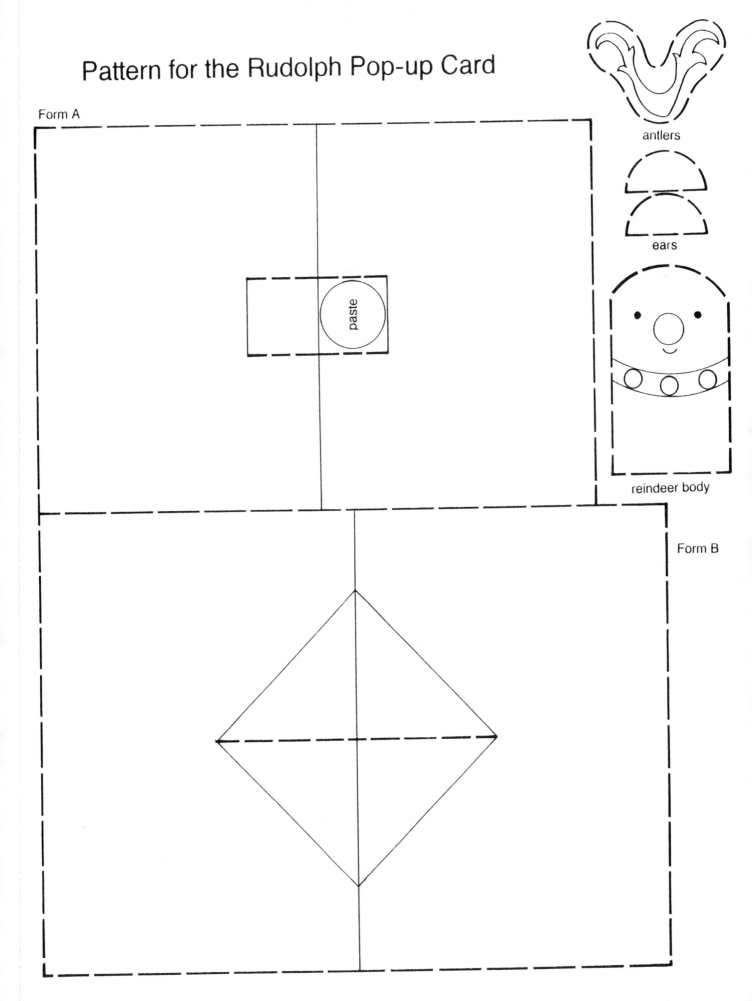

Form A

paste

Form B

antlers

ears

reindeer body

Cross-Legged Elf

Create a delightful little elf to stand on your desk. Add a little imagination to the basic shape to create other characters of your own.

Materials:
- Construction paper
    - green or red — 9″ x 9″-body
        - 3″ x 3″-hat
    - white — 3″ x 3″-face
        - 1″ x 3″-hands and collar
    - black — 1″ x 3″-hair
- Scissors, paste, crayons
- Stapler

Steps to follow:

1. Fold the basic body piece.

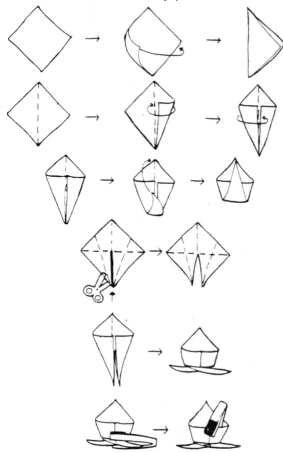

2. Cut out the other parts and paste to the basic body shape.

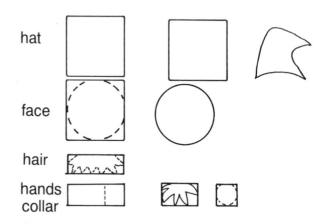

Curl the elf's toes.

3. What will you put in the elf's pocket?
   Spelling words?
   A snack?
   Christmas wishes?

Draw an Elf or a Toy Soldier

These basic drawing suggestions are just a beginning. Allow students time to improvise, change and develop their own Christmas characters after you have drawn together and established the basic steps with everyone. Eliminate the phrase— "I don't know how to draw it!"

An elf

A toy soldier

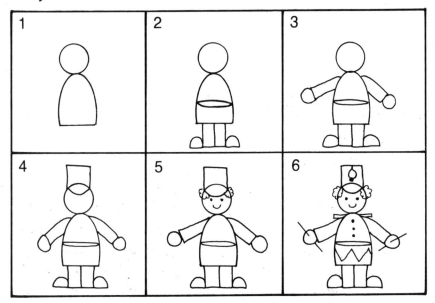

Now draw the elf and toy soldier again. This time try to make it appear that its knees are bent or that its arms are held up.

Why not risk it all and see if you can draw a side view of these characters. You can begin with the very same basic shapes.

A Christmas Angel

(to hang on your tree)

Reproduce the angel pattern on page 23. Add your special touches to make her sparkle on your tree.

Steps to follow:

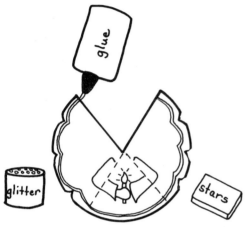

1. Color the angel and her candle.
2. Cut on the heavy dotted lines. Fold on the light dotted lines.
3. Add a line of glue and glitter to the lower edge. Lick and stick stars can also make a nice border.

4. Draw a face on the angel's head. Put a glitter halo in her hair. Glue the head to the body.

5. Punch a hole through the top of the wings and thread a strip of yarn through. Tie a loop. The yarn will hold the angel together and allow you to hang it on the tree.

Christmas Angel Pattern

paste

Santa Paper Doll

Dress this Santa for any occasion. What would he wear to a swimming party, to an Easter egg hunt, or to the zoo? What does he wear when he and Mrs. Santa work in the garden? Is red his favorite color or does he just prefer it in the winter?

Reproduce the Santa paper doll pattern on page 25. Use construction paper or card stock. Children may color and cut it out. Now they are ready to create his wardrobe.

Steps to follow:

1. Tape the paper doll to a window.
2. Tape white paper over it so you can see the doll shape through the paper. Draw the piece of clothing to fit Santa.
3. Color the clothing and add tabs so the clothes will stay on the paper doll. Cut out the clothing.
4. Dress Santa in his new outfit and explain to a friend why you made that choice.

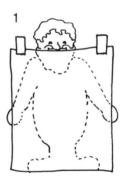

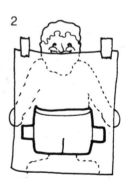

Santa Paper Doll Pattern

25

Draw Santa, His Reindeer, and His Sleigh

Follow the steps to create pictures of Santa, his reindeer, and his sleigh. Do the first drawings together, so that your students are comfortable with the basic forms. Encourage them to think of interesting backgrounds.

Santa

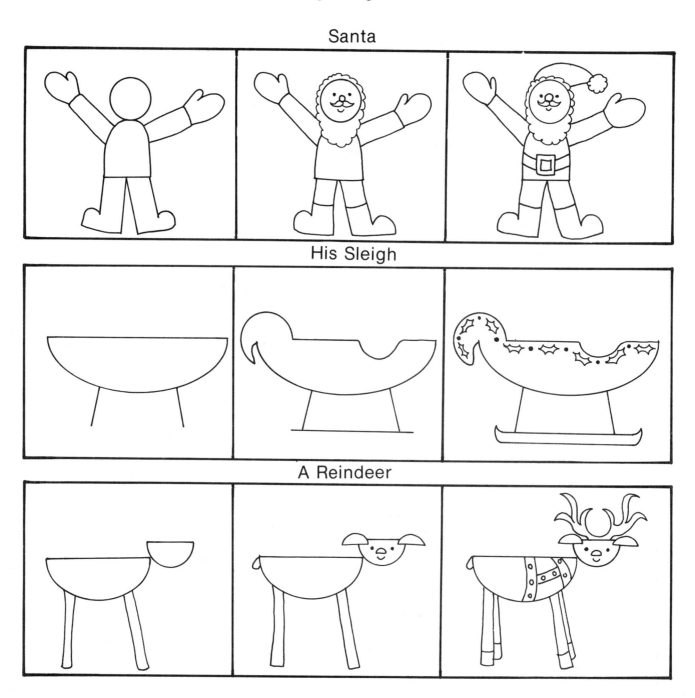

His Sleigh

A Reindeer

Now, let the children create their own pictures by placing the three drawings in interesting arrangements and using their imaginations to create an appropriate background.

Are there packages in the sleigh? Is the reindeer pulling the sleigh to the top of a house? Does Santa have his pack flung over his shoulder?

Encourage your students to make their pictures tell a story.

Festive Thumb Prints

The materials needed for this activity are close at hand! Pull out a fresh stamp pad and get your fingers ready to press into service! Experiment with shapes and designs on newsprint before making a finished product.

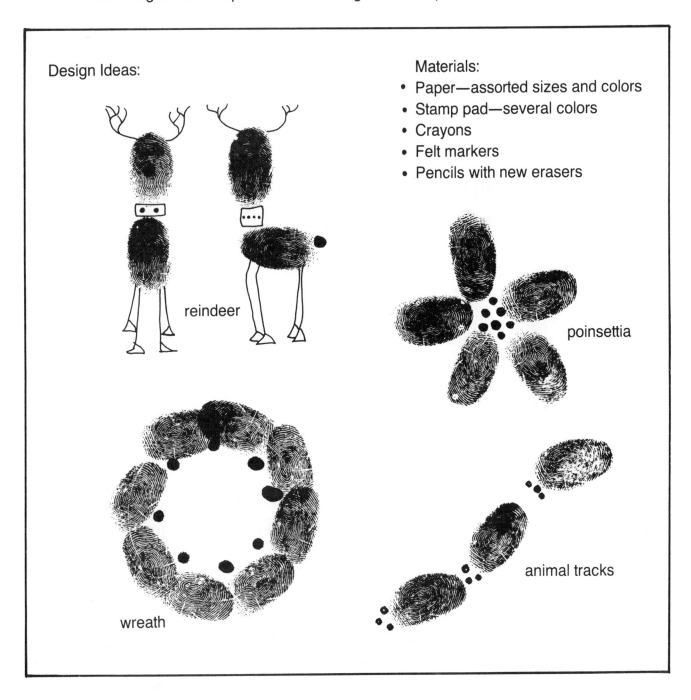

Design Ideas:

reindeer

poinsettia

wreath

animal tracks

Materials:
- Paper—assorted sizes and colors
- Stamp pad—several colors
- Crayons
- Felt markers
- Pencils with new erasers

These thumb print designs are clever Christmas card illustrations. They may also be used successfully as border designs for framing Christmas stories. Use colored stamp pads for festive results. Crayons or fine point felt markers can be used to add details. The rubber eraser on a pencil makes a useful stamp for eyes, berries, etc.

A Remarkable Candy Cane

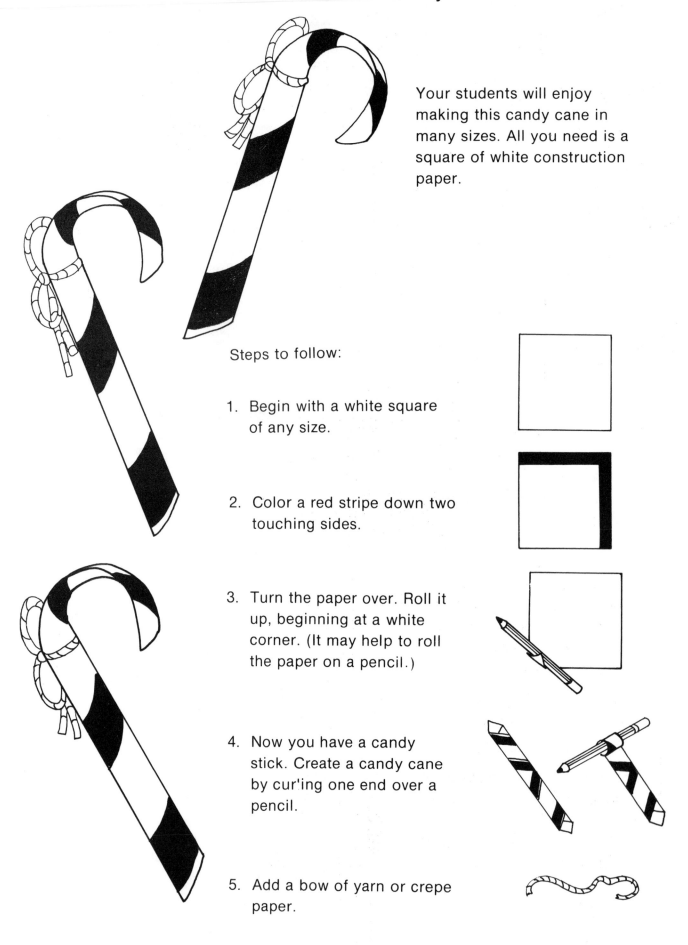

Your students will enjoy making this candy cane in many sizes. All you need is a square of white construction paper.

Steps to follow:

1. Begin with a white square of any size.

2. Color a red stripe down two touching sides.

3. Turn the paper over. Roll it up, beginning at a white corner. (It may help to roll the paper on a pencil.)

4. Now you have a candy stick. Create a candy cane by cur'ing one end over a pencil.

5. Add a bow of yarn or crepe paper.

Snowman

Create this snowman with white sponge painting on blue construction paper. He will really sparkle if you sprinkle a small amount of silver glitter on the wet paint.

Steps to follow:

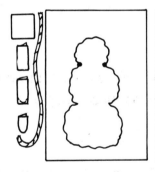

1. Sponge paint the snowman shape.

2. Poke two holes to thread yarn through. Cut mittens from folded construction paper and glue to the ends of the yarn.

3. Use construction paper scraps or found objects (buttons, cloth, beans, beads, popcorn) to create a face, hat and buttons for the snowman.

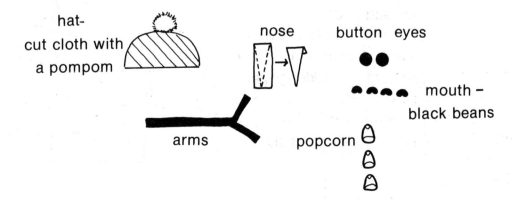

hat-
cut cloth with
a pompom

nose

button eyes

●●

mouth –
black beans

arms

popcorn

Penguins Sliding to the Sea

Watch these penguins slide down the ice floe. Children enjoy the three-dimensional effect.

Materials:
- White construction paper
    9″ x 12″ for background
    2″ x 3½″ for penguin bodies
- Orange scraps for beaks
- Black scraps for wings
- Blue tissue strips
    2″ x 9″ for water
- Crayons, paste, scissors
- Liquid starch

Steps to follow:

1. Use a black crayon to outline the ice floe. (Older students can brush the paper with liquid starch and lay one sheet of pale blue tissue over the whole page to represent an ice floe. Let dry, then draw with black crayon.)

2. Cut wave lines on top edge of tissue strips. Adhere one or two strips of tissue with brushed-on liquid starch. Allow the blue tint to smear up onto the snow slide. Let the background dry.

3. Prepare the penguins by rounding off the top corners of the white rectangles. Fold up the edge approximately ½″. Draw the basic penguin design on your rounded shape.

Cut out an orange scrap for a beak. Fold the back edge. Paste that edge to the penguin.
Cut two small black rectangles for wings. Round one end of each wing. Paste wings to your bird.

4. Paste the lower edge of the penguins to the ice floe.

Polar Bear and Eskimo Puppets

Put the Eskimo on one hand and the polar bear on the other. Now you're ready to share what you've learned about their homeland. Or you might want to create an adventure for the two characters to act out.

Materials:
- Reproduce the pattern on the following page.
- White construction paper for puppet backs and snowball.
- Crayons, scissors, glue

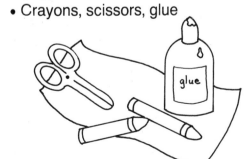

Steps to follow:

1. Polar Bear
   Cut out the bear pattern. Cut a back from white construction paper to match the front piece. Glue around the edges leaving the bottom open. Fringe the ears and bottom to give him that ragged, furry look.

2. Eskimo
   Cut out the Eskimo pattern. Cut a back from white paper to match the front. Glue around the outside edge, leaving the bottom open. Fringe around the top of the Eskimo's hood. Color the Eskimo's face and clothing. Cut out a snowball and glue it in Eskimo's mittens.

Polar Bear and Eskimo Puppet Patterns

Cut a back to match each of these puppets.

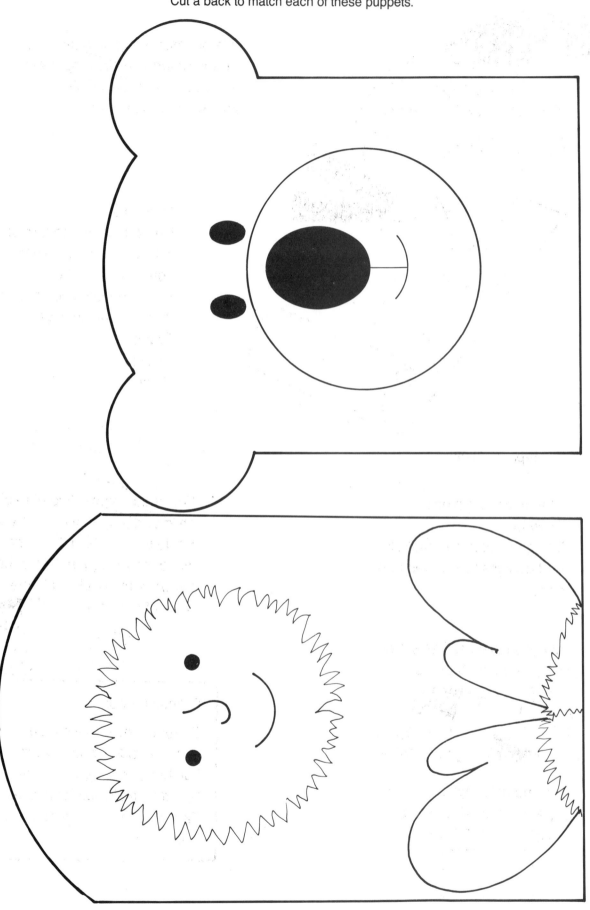

3-D Christmas Trees

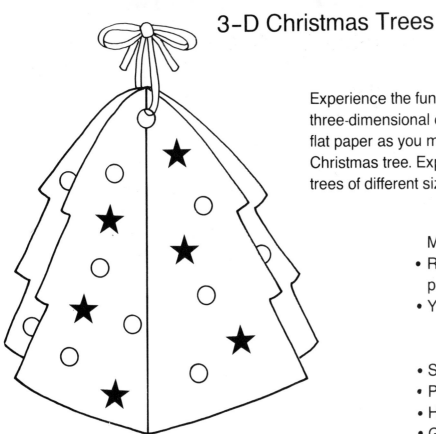

Experience the fun of creating three-dimensional objects from flat paper as you make this Christmas tree. Experiment with trees of different sizes and colors.

Materials:
- Reproduce the pattern on this page using construction paper.
- You'll need 4 per tree.
    (Older students may prefer to create their own tree shapes.)
- Scissors
- Paste or glue
- Hole punch
- Glitter, paint, crayons
- Yarn (6" strips)

1. Cut out and fold the four pattern pieces down the middle.

2. Apply paste to one side of one folded tree. Place another folded tree on thie pasted area. Now paste the top layer of this tree. Place the next tree on the paste. Repeat with the last tree section. Now paste the two open ends together. Your tree stands up!

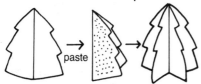

3. Punch a hole in the top of the tree. Put yarn through the hole and tie it in a loop.

4. Decorate the tree:
    Punch holes with a hole punch.
    Add silver or gold stars.

You need 4 copies of this pattern for each tree.

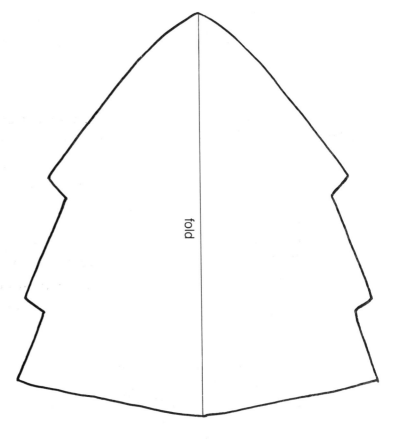

fold

Origami Christmas Ornaments

Turn simple squares of colored paper into charming ornaments for your Christmas tree. If you paste them to paper, they become greeting cards for your special friends.

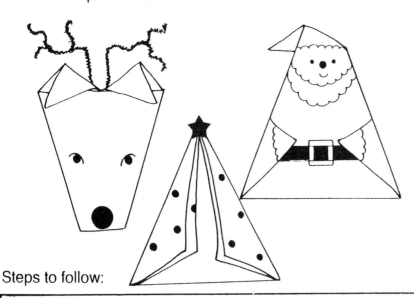

Materials:
- Lightweight colored paper

  brown ⎫
  green ⎬ 4″ or 6″
  red   ⎭ squares
- Pipe cleaners to cut and bend for antlers
- Crayons or felt markers
- Glitter
- Glue

Steps to follow: Finishing Touches

Reindeer	
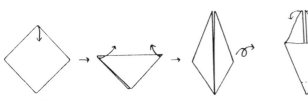	a. Bend pipe cleaner pieces for antlers. Glue on to head. b. Draw eyes with crayons or felt pens. c. Add glue to nose and sprinkle with glitter.

Christmas Tree	
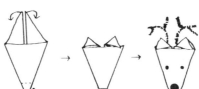 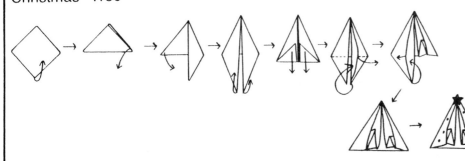	a. Draw, print, or paste ornaments on your tree. b. Add a shiny star to the top. c. You can open the tree up and write a message inside.

Santa in Chimney	
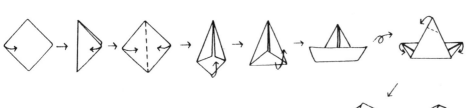 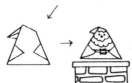	a. Draw Santa's face, belt, and hands with crayons or felt pens. b. Paste Santa inside a chimney. c. Draw bricks on the chimney.

30

Dragon Headband
Wear it to celebrate Chinese New Year.

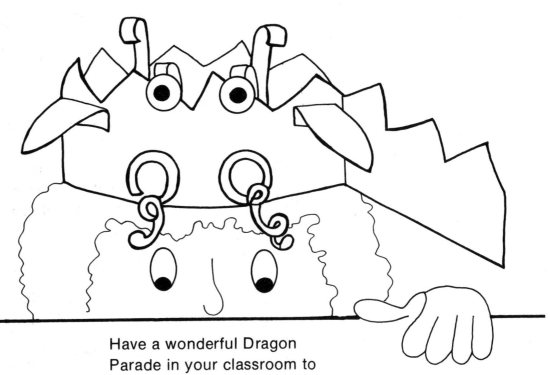

Have a wonderful Dragon
Parade in your classroom to
celebrate Chinese New Year.
Everyone can wear this
delightful dragon headband.

Steps to follow:

1. Cut a 12" x 18" sheet of
   green construction paper in
   zigzag cuts down the center
   of the paper.
2. Glue these pieces together
   to form the dragon.
3. Staple the headband to fit
   each student. Let the left-
   over hang down to become
   the dragon's tail.
4. Cut the rest of the dragon
   from colorful scraps of
   construction paper. Yellow,
   magenta and orange are
   good choices.

   Glue these pieces to the
   dragon.

   Enjoy your parade!

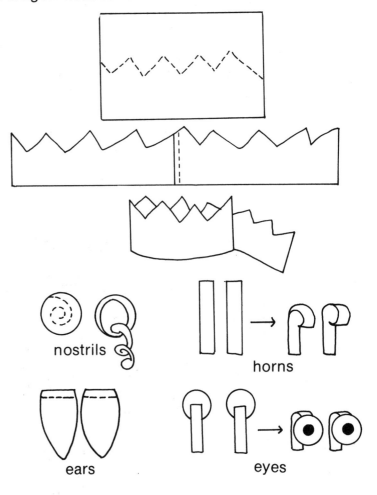

nostrils

horns

ears

eyes

Furnish Groundhog's Burrow

Set imagination to work to decorate the interior of groundhog's burrow. Start with an empty shoe box and see what develops.

Materials:
- Brown construction paper
  2" x 4" — groundhog
- Shoe or other small box
- Assorted odds and ends of paper and cloth
  wallpaper, wrapping paper, tinfoil, burlap, etc.
- Green tissue paper squares
  1" x 1"
- Glue, scissors, crayons, felt pens
- Exacto knife

Steps to follow:

1. Cut a 2¼" slit in one side of the box with the Exacto knife. (This becomes the top of the burrow.)
2. Make groundhog from the brown construction paper.
3. Color the top of the box with tissue paper "grass." Wrap tissue over pencil eraser, dip in glue and set on box.
4. Let students use their own imaginations to furnish groundhog's home.
   They might enjoy taking the project home to finish, then bringing it back to unveil the completed project.

put in the slit

tissue

Groundhog Puppet

February 2 is Groundhog day.

What fun to watch groundhog peek out of his hole. Use the puppet to reinforce all the information you teach about the significance of Groundhog Day.

Materials:
- Reproduce the patterns on this and the following page.
- Tongue depressor
- Crayons, scissors, paste
- Stapler

Steps to follow:

1. Cut the dotted lines to create grass. Cut the slit on the fold line. Fold up on the line. Staple the sides.
Now color the sun yellow and the grass green.

2. Cut out the cloud. Decide if it will cover part of the sun or not. Paste it in place.

3. Color, then cut out the groundhog. Paste him to a tongue depressor. Slip the other end of the tongue depressor through the slit. Make sure the groundhog pops up and down.

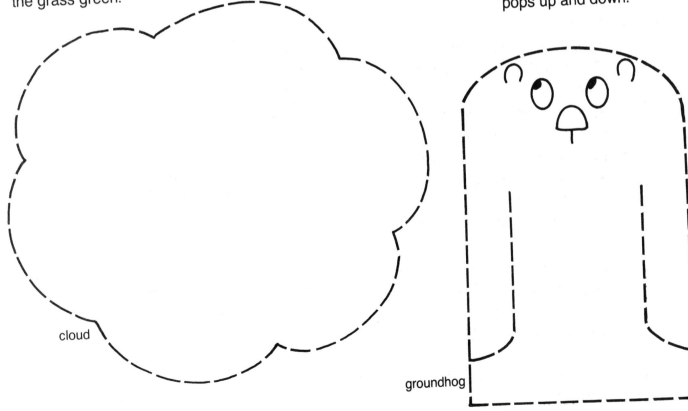

cloud

groundhog

February 2 is Groundhog Day.

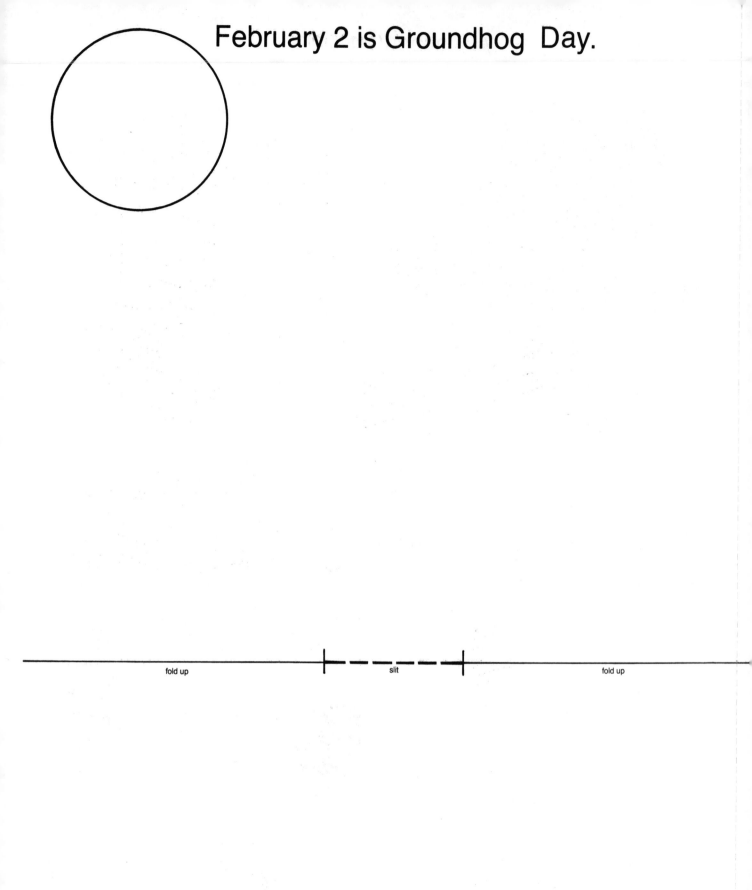

fold up   slit   fold up

34

A Woven Valentine

Create a charming woven Valentine. It can be used for a greeting card, a basket for a small treat, or an ornament to hang on a tree.

Materials to use:
- Reproduce the pattern on the next page on white construction paper (OR on two shades of colored paper).
- Scissors
- Paste
- Crayons

Steps to follow:

1. Color the Valentine pieces; one section dark, one section light. Cut out on the dotted lines.
2. Fold over and weave each strip over and under.
3. Paste the loose edges down.

For a greeting card:
Open and write your message inside. Give to a special friend.

As a basket or ornament:
Paste the sides together, leaving the top open. Add a handle of construction paper.

Tuck a little treat or gift inside.

OR...
Make your basket in red and green to hang on your Christmas tree.

Pattern for a Woven Valentine

Run on construction paper.
Cut on dotted lines.

fold

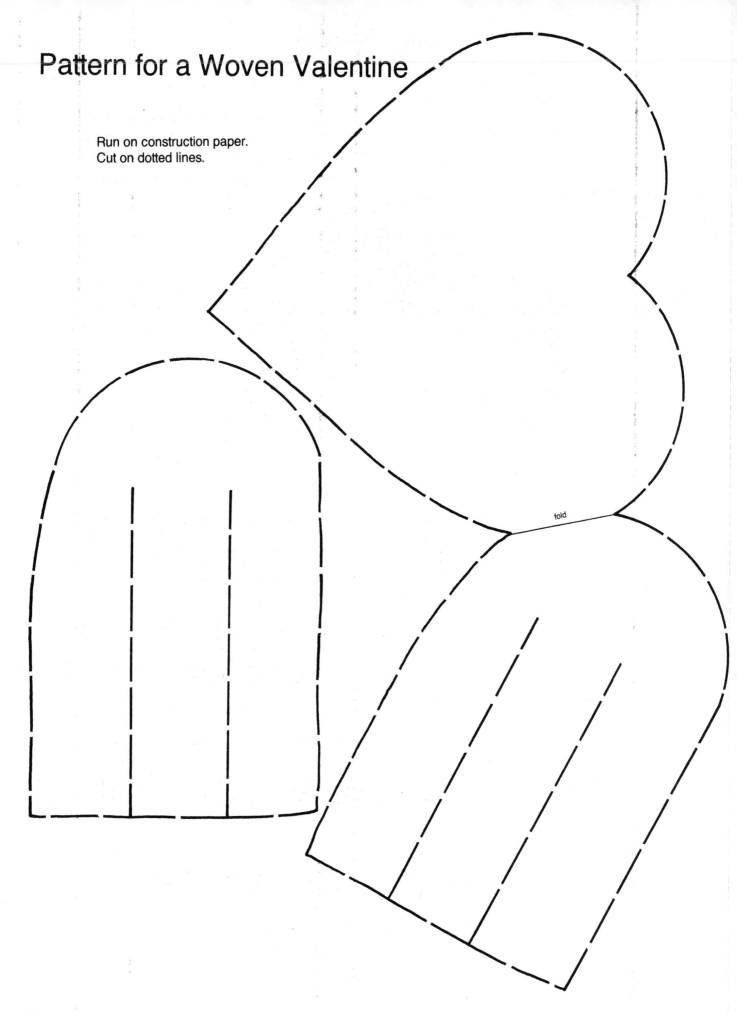

Heart Baskets

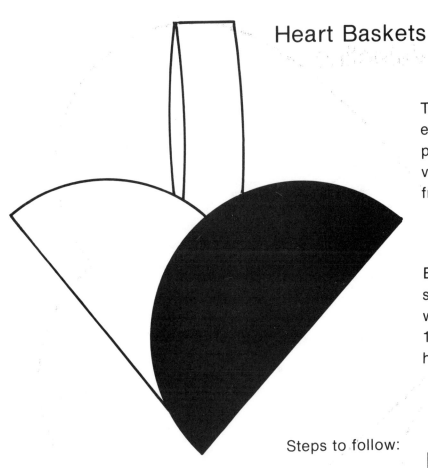

These delightful baskets are easy to create from construction paper. They will hold a small valentine treat for a special friend.

Each student will need two 4" squares, one red or pink and one white. They each will also need a 1" X 9" strip of red or pink for a handle.

Steps to follow:

1. Round off the corners of each square to form circles.

2. Fold each circle in half.

3. Put the two circles together as illustrated and paste the outside pieces together.

4. Paste the handle on the basket.

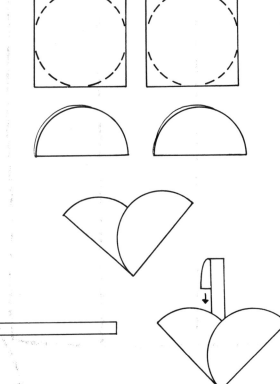

Note: You can use the same pattern to create Christmas ornaments. Make the circles from green and red squares.

Origami Valentine Pocket

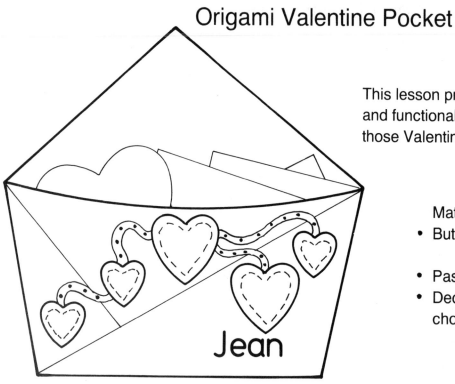

This lesson provides an attractive and functional way to pass out those Valentine cards in class.

Materials:
- Butcher paper, any color 22" x 22" square
- Paste
- Decorative supplies of your choice

Steps to follow:

1. Fold the butcher paper.

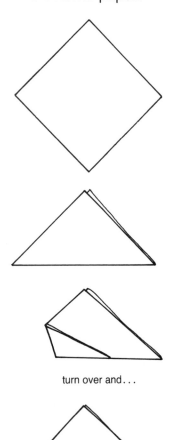

turn over and. . .

2. Tuck in the top flap between the folded sheets.
   Turn it over and tuck in the flap on the other side. (or leave it out to act as a closing flap which can be taped to the student's desk) .

3. Decorate your Valentine pocket in your favorite style. They are striking when printed with heart-shaped sponges in bright colored paint. Glitter, doilies, ribbons and lace are always wonderful additions.
   The pockets can be pinned along a wall or to a bulletin board for easy distribution of Valentine cards.

Heart Chain Links

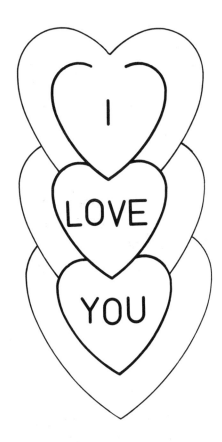

Long or short, this Valentine makes an exciting, versatile activity.

Materials:
- Construction paper square 4" x 4" is a good size in various colors
- Scissors, felt pens, pencils

Steps to follow:

1. Fold the square in half. Hold on the fold and cut half a heart. (Younger students may need a pattern.)
   Cut a smaller heart on the inside, but stop before going all the way around.

2. Intertwine one heart with the next by slipping the heart point under the small inner heart of the next Valentine.

3. Now create a Valentine surprise.
   - Hang chains in the window.
   - Create a message by writing one letter on each heart. Disassemble and give to a friend.
   - Alternate colors (maybe each color in the rainbow).
   - Curl the center or decorate the edges.

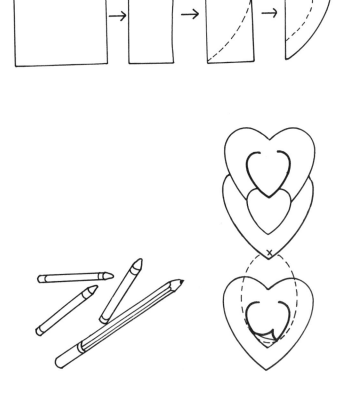

Pop-Up Valentines

What fun to receive a 3-dimensional Valentine greeting. Use this easy pop-up form to create a flock of special wishes for friends.

Materials:
- Reproduce the pattern on the following page.
- Construction paper
    9" x 7" — cover
- Paper scraps
- Paste, scissors
- Felt pens or crayons

Steps to follow:

1. Cut out your pattern page. Cut and fold the bird's beak.

2. Draw and color your Valentine bird. Add special touches with paper scraps.

3. Paste the bird into its cover. Put paste around edges only. Be sure the center folds touch exactly.

4. Write a Valentine message or poem on your card. Send it to a friend.

Pop-Up Valentine Pattern

EVAN-MOOR CORP., 1986

1. Cut out pattern and fold in half.

2. Cut on dotted line.

3. Open the paper and reverse the folds by pushing them to the inside.

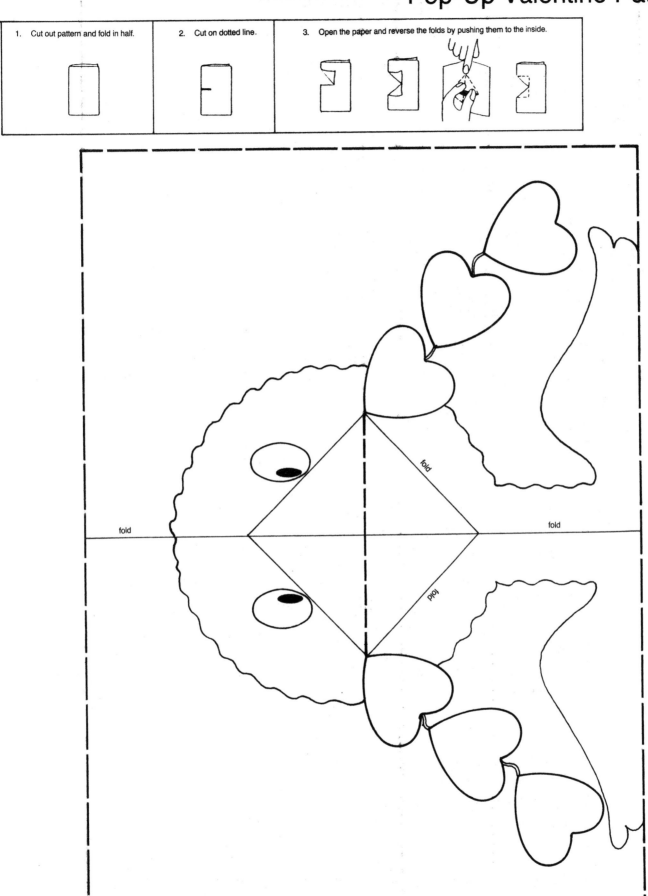

fold

fold

fold

fold

WINTER ART

Valentine Mouse Book Mark

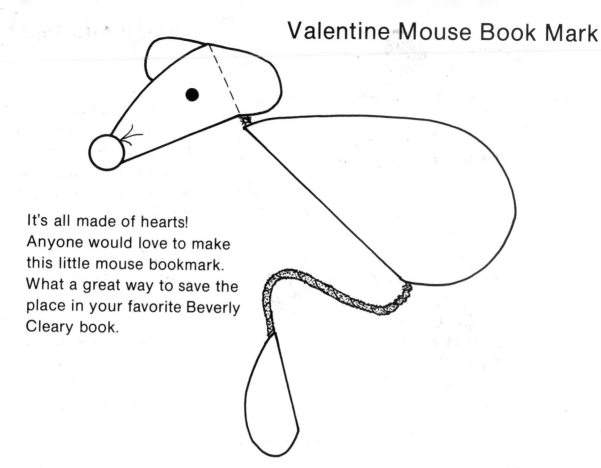

It's all made of hearts! Anyone would love to make this little mouse bookmark. What a great way to save the place in your favorite Beverly Cleary book.

Steps to follow:

1. Begin with a 7" x 3" piece of white construction paper.

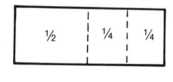

fold and cut

2. Cut hearts on the fold.

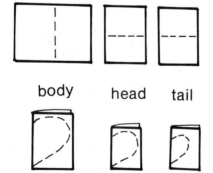

body   head   tail

3. Paste the yarn in the center of the hearts.

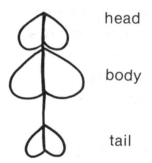

head

body

tail

Fold and paste the hearts shut.

4. Head:
   Add a pink circle for a nose, a black dot on both sides for eyes, and lines for little whiskers.
   Fold the round ears forward.

Heart Art—Part I

This activity provides exploration of the media of cut paper using the topic of hearts. Students are provided with an overview of techniques, then given time to explore the possibilities.

Materials:
- Newsprint
- Construction paper
  assorted sizes
  Valentine colors
- Scissors, pencil
- Hole punch

Steps to follow:

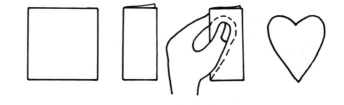

1. A heart needs to be symmetrical, so first teach students an easy way to cut a heart.
   Practice on newsprint until students perfect the process. Then use colored construction paper. Use squares approximately 4″ by 4″.

2. Experiment with making:
   - Tiny Valentines
   - Fat Valentines
   - Cut a heart within a heart
   - Cut and peel open the center
   - Punch holes in your heart
   - A broken heart (cut apart)
   - A heart with slits
   - A pleated heart

Save all these hearts and pin them up as a border for a February bulletin board or use them to create special Valentines for friends.

Heart Art—Part II

Put all the skill in designing hearts you accumulated in Part I of Heart Art into the creation of "heart-y" characters.

There are no steps to follow.
Here are some ideas to share with your students. They will generate many others with their own imaginations.

Materials:
- Construction paper assorted sizes and colors
- Lace doilies, ribbons, pipe cleaners, tinfoil, glitter, etc.
- Scissors, paste, crayons, felt pens
- Stapler, hole punch

Draw the Presidents

Follow these steps to create the perfect illustration for
your reports on Lincoln and Washington.

George Washington

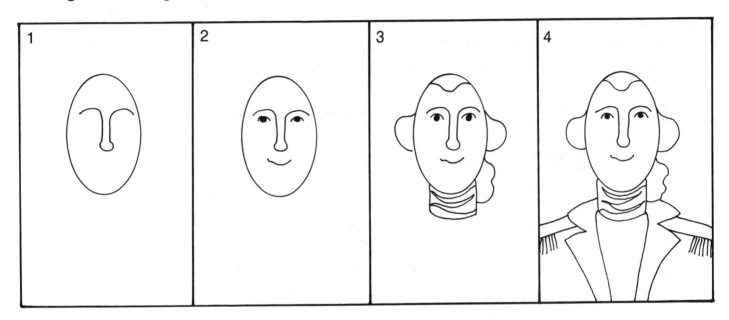

Abraham Lincoln

Abraham Lincoln's Log Cabin

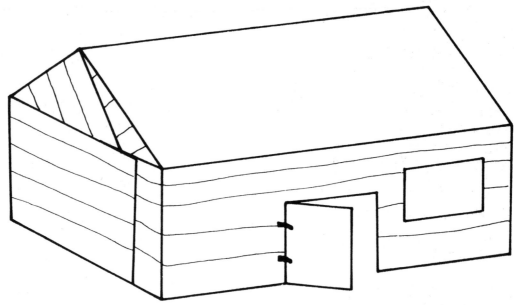

Materials:
- Brown construction paper
     9″ x 12″
- Scissors
- Black crayon
- Paste

Made from one piece of construction paper, this free-standing log cabin is one you'll use again and again. Why not combine all of the students' cabins to create a whole village.

Steps to follow:

1. Fold paper into 16 boxes.
   (Fold in half 4 times.)

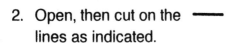

2. Open, then cut on the — lines as indicated.

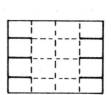

3. Draw logs, door, and window.

   Cut door and fold open.
   Cut out window.

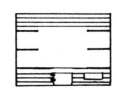

   Fold into a standing position by overlapping cut ends. Paste ends in place.

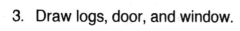